YEHUDHITH

PHOTOGRAPHS BY ELLIOT ROSS

with texts about
women and the Holocaust

Introduction by Ellen Ullman

hawkhaven press
san francisco

For my mother Nancy Koenigsberg Ross
and to the memory of Stacey Sussman

Transliterated from Hebrew, the female name Yehudhith (yeh·hoo·DEET)
is the origin of the English name Judith. Yehudhith's various meanings
include "woman of Judah" and "Jewish woman."

Photographs copyright © 2004 by Elliot Ross
Introduction copyright © 2004 by Ellen Ullman

First published in the United States in 2004 by hawkhaven press
1915 Funston Ave., San Francisco, California 94116.

ISBN 0-9666917-9-2.

All proceeds from the sale of *Yehudhith* will go toward the establishment of
the Charlotte Salomon Award for Visual Artists at the Jewish Museum San Francisco.

As Out of Smoke: The Women of Elliot Ross's *Yehudhith*

It is an odd way for a Jewish man to begin a book about the Holocaust: with a quote from Adolf Hitler. But so begins Elliot Ross's collection of photographs, *Yehudhith*, with a picture of a woman holding a violin and, facing her, a quote from *Mein Kampf*—Hitler musing (horribly) about the Jews who had lived in Linz, Austria for centuries, becoming what Hitler calls "Europeanized," taking on "a human look," until, he says, "even I took them for Germans."

And, indeed, the woman in Ross's photograph does look German. She is blond, fair-skinned, strong-chinned. The violin and bow she holds are veritable signifiers of high *Mittel Europa* culture at the turn of the last century. We can imagine her as the daughter of a prosperous burgher of Linz, the city that welcomed Hitler so joyously into its main square, our violin player posing for her portrait just before Herr Professor arrives for her music lesson. If she is a Jewish woman, we, like Hitler, cannot tell; there is nothing of the stereotyped Ashkenazi about her. As we look at her image, we're not certain what to think or feel, except discomfort. Who is she?

It is only when we turn the page that we begin to understand the story Ross is about to tell in words and pictures. For the next photograph is an answer to the first, another woman, this one unmistakably Jewish (presumably one whom Hitler considered non-human in appearance). She is strongly beautiful, almost classically Semitic, something about her inviting the dangerous phrase "beautiful Jewess." Yet we can't enjoy her beauty for long. For the text paired with this image, from the scholar Mary Lowenthal Felstiner, tells us the Nazi view of women: "cell-bearers," lowest ranking members of the low antirace of Jews, despised for having spawned it. Again we hear from Hitler: "Every child that a woman brings into the world is a battle, a battle waged for the existence of her people." And we begin to understand that we are about to get a very particular view of the Holocaust: as a battle over the bodies of women—mothers and potential mothers, as the Nazis saw them—the special horrors afforded them as living emblems of the survival of the Jewish people.

What follows then is the almost unbearable story of what the women endured: rape, physical degradation, spiritual assault, murder. Elliot Ross has culled the literature of the Holocaust, the writings of survivors and scholars, to find the experience from the women's point of view, offering us excerpts that recount the horrors suffered by pregnant women, mothers, daughters, old women, sisters, in the ghettos and death camps. Even the stories of heroism—and there are many, an entire section devoted to women who resisted the Gestapo and SS with unimaginable courage—cannot save us from the grimness of this vision. Ross is too knowledgeable about the real oppressions of the Holocaust to let us get away with anything so simple as an idealized image of undying courage in the face of brutality. The penultimate excerpt in the book reminds us that the Nazis "engineered a system deliberately designed to make heroism virtually impossible." The message is too clear: "To expect heroism from victims or to romantically attribute it to them is to treat the Holocaust as if it were a character test, rather than a program of systematic dehumanization."

Why then do I say that the story of what these women endured is "almost unbearable?" Where is the "almost" that lets us enter into the experiences of these women? For I take it as a tenet of Holocaust art that we, the viewers, must be offered a way into the experience, and this entryway must involve saving us from utter despair. There is no moral uplift in the story of the Holocaust; Cynthia Ozick's famous essay about Anne Frank is right: it is dishonest to take out of context Anne's desire to believe that people, at heart, are good. Quite the contrary, as the book's penultimate quote tells us, the Shoah is a vision of life with the human values torn out, where hope is impossible.

What in *Yehudhith*, then, saves us from this despair? The answer is the photographs. For Elliot Ross has not photographed women who suffered the degradations of the Holocaust; he has not shown us grizzled survivors. Though the women in his photographs seem to exist somewhat out of time, we can tell they are our contemporaries – women who *might* have been the subjects of such brutality, but were not. They are the age of the women the SS might have separated out from the transports, beaten, then thrown still living into the crematory, as one quote tells us. But this did not happen to the women we're looking at. These Jewish women are very much alive, intact, unbroken.

All the same, the darkness shadows them, literally. The images are somber, eclipsed. Photographically speaking, they spend most of their time in what is called the "toe" portion of the film, that part of the emulsion that reacts less actively to lower light levels, producing thinly shaded tones in the negative and deep grays in the print, which appear in slow, near gradation to one another—the opposite of the modern "snappy" high-contrast print. One could say that the darkness is the subject of these photographs, as much as are the women themselves. Moral blackness, fog, crematory ash—all these seem to be waiting in the dim areas of the frames. The women's faces and bodies emerge as out of smoke.

Surrounded by darkness, the women remain at a remove. They do not insist that we engage them personally; some do not even look at us at all. They seem involved in some inner gaze, to exist elsewhere, else *time*. Unmoored from the present, they are simultaneously contemporaries and women who lived sixty years ago—at once children of the safe American century and precarious residents of Linz in 1940. Their images are pictures of our sisters, friends, and young mothers and, at the same time, darkening photographs of lives just about to be lost.

What lets Ross achieve this rich confounding of time is his use of a resurrected pictorialism, that nineteenth-century photographic movement that treated its subjects as symbols or illustrations, for instance a Julia Margaret Cameron photograph in which a child is not to be seen as any actual girl or boy, but as an emblem of childhood. Ross's pictorialism is only suggested; the women are not illustrations, strictly speaking. They are not stand-ins for the women discussed in the quoted passages that accompany the images. Still, his technique allows us to imagine them as, if not the actual women, then their descendants. Where nineteenth-century pictorialism used soft focus, Ross uses darkness, profile, the women often presented in silhouetted cameo, as still and calm as a figure on a brooch. Then, breaking through his own consciously distancing technique, Ross will insert the image of a face in strong, direct gaze, and we are shocked back from any temptation to dally in daydreaming. Something strange happens to time: the contemporary women are cast backward into the horrors of the past, and the awful words describing the Holocaust, in all their brutality, are thrown forward at us.

It is this dual time sense that both allows us to enter into the experience of the Holocaust—feel it—while not drowning. We can imagine the sufferings imposed on women who were very much like those in the photographs; meanwhile the pictorialist motive, with its Apollonian remove, asserts a stubborn kind of classicism, a refusal to let the Holocaust take away the human longing for beauty. Ross quotes Lawrence Langer saying, "Among the many victims of the Holocaust was the classical idea of the beauty of the human form. Humiliated memory testifies to the erosion of that ideal." In this context, Ross's pictorialism, his almost palpable yearning for an iconic image of the Jewish woman, is an audacious act.

The problem of what is called "Holocaust art," finally, is one of time. How do we keep fresh the memory of something that recedes from us continually? Soon there will be no one alive who can remember it from actual experience; from here forward, our task will be to find mnemonics, to experience the Shoah not in memory but in imagination. Artists' choices of mnemonics will be controversial, necessarily so, since their images will come from contemporary experience, lacking the authority of "the true" and the sanctity of testimony. The problem will be to find that particular experience that *ignites* the Holocaust in the individual artist, the trigger that tells him or her exactly what was lost, individually, personally. For Elliot Ross, it was the loss of a woman friend to cancer. From there, he considered the other young Jewish women he knew; and it all ignited a chain of feeling, from one individual, to the women around him, to the realization of what the Holocaust had taken away from him, and from all of us: an entire generation of Jewish women. In *Yehudhith*, he lets us travel with him through the images that connect him, and ultimately us, to the Holocaust, to the "battle waged for the existence of her people."

Ellen Ullman
San Francisco, California

YEHUDHITH

YOUR LOVE CIRCLES ABOVE ME
LIKE HUMAN SMOKE ABOVE THE WIND

TADEUSZ BOROWSKI
Farewell to Maria

...FOR LOVE IS STRONG AS DEATH...

The Song of Solomon

There were few Jews in Linz. In the course of the centuries their outward appearance had become Europeanized and had taken on a human look; in fact, I even took them for Germans.

ADOLF HITLER
Mein Kampf

It was the Nazi view of all women as cell-bearers that condemned the Jewish ones. Even within the lowest life-form—the antirace—women ranked lower still, for spawning it. In Hitler's cliché, "Every child that a woman brings into the world is a battle, a battle waged for the existence of her people." Because women in their biology held history hereafter, one gestating Jewish mother posed a greater threat than any fighting man.

MARY LOWENTHAL FELSTINER
To Paint Her Life: Charlotte Salomon in the Nazi Era

THE WOMEN WERE HERDED INTO A BARRACK, WHERE, ONE AFTER THE OTHER, THEY HAD TO LIE DOWN ON THE TABLE FOR EXAMINATION. THE CAMP DOCTOR, A PRISONER, STUCK HER FINGERS INTO THE VAGINA AND THE RECTUM TO SEARCH FOR EMBRYOS AND VALUABLES, BOTH OF WHICH MEANT DEATH.

CORDELIA EDVARDSON
Burned Child Seeks Fire

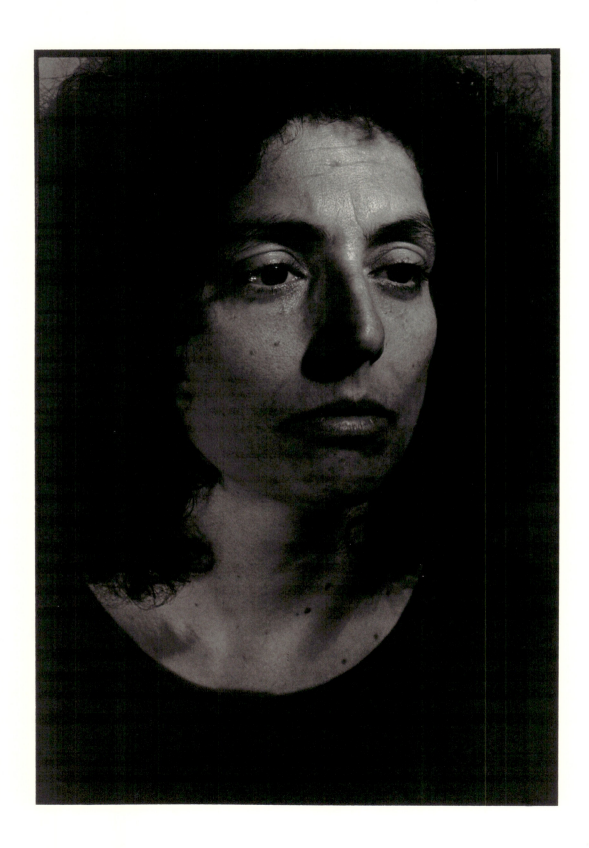

One day I happened to have an errand near the crematories and saw with my own eyes what was done to these [pregnant] women.

They were surrounded by a group of SS men and women, who amused themselves by giving these helpless creatures a taste of hell.... They were beaten with clubs and whips, torn by dogs, dragged around by the hair and kicked in the stomach with heavy German boots. Then, when they collapsed, they were thrown into the crematory—alive.

GISELLA PERL
I Was a Doctor in Auschwitz

It was usually the young and strong who were selected for work. The old, the weak, and the very young were immediately killed.

Ruth Bestman remembers walking with a group of prisoners in Auschwitz. Among them was a woman with her two daughters. "One said 'Mother' in Polish. The Germans heard that and knew the woman was much older than the rest of us. They took her right out to the gas chambers."

DAVID A. ADLER
We Remember the Holocaust

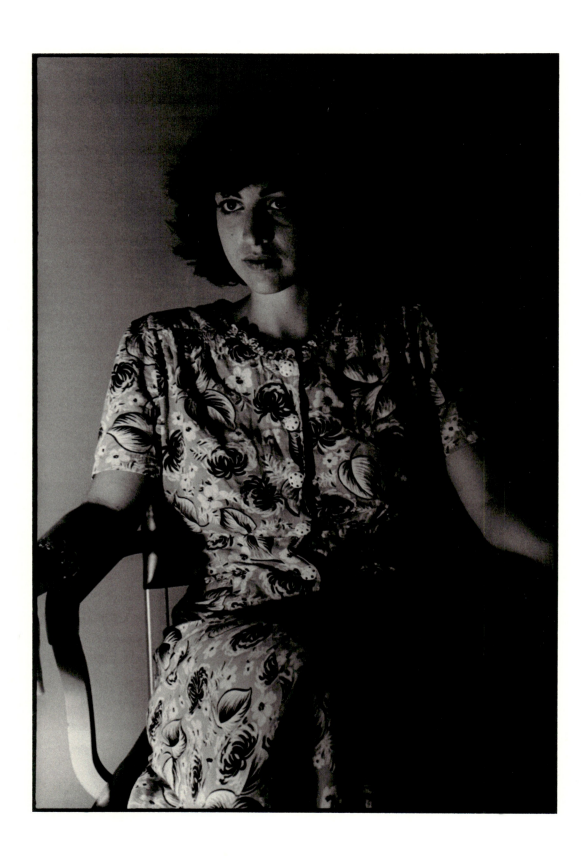

JEWISH WOMEN ARE THE TARGETS OF NAZIS BECAUSE
THEY ARE JEWS, BUT THEY ARE ATTACKED AND USED AS
WOMEN — AS MOTHERS, AS OBJECTS OF SEXUAL DERI-
SION AND EXPLOITATION, AS PERSONS LESS VALUABLE
THAN MEN....

JOAN RINGELHEIM
"Thoughts About Women and the Holocaust"

JEWISH WOMEN, PARTICULARLY OBSERVANT JEWISH WOMEN, WERE SUBJECT TO STILL ANOTHER LEVEL OF ABUSE. JUDAISM SEPARATES RELIGIOUS WOMEN FROM ADULT MEN…AND PLACES VERY HIGH VALUES ON CHASTITY, MODESTY, AND OBEDIENCE. IN THE HANDS OF THE NAZIS, OBSERVANT WOMEN WERE, THEREFORE, PARTICULARLY DEFENSELESS AGAINST THE ASTONISHING RANGE OF DEGRADATIONS: VERBAL ABUSE, UNTENDED MENSTRUATION, PUBLIC NAKEDNESS, HEAD AND BODY SHAVINGS BY MEN, AND INTERNAL BODY SEARCHES.

MYRNA GOLDENBERG
"Different Horrors, Same Hell:
Women Remembering the Holocaust"

When human beings ceased to be emissaries or legatees of love and became instead agents or victims of power on such a massive scale, we may have witnessed a shift in civilization's priorities....

LAWRENCE L. LANGER
Holocaust Testimonies: The Ruins of Memory

"Where has she gone?"

"If you must know, my brother and sister and I turned her in last night. The police came and took her away."

"You did such a thing? Why?"

"She's a Jew. Isn't that enough? All these years and we didn't know it. It was my father who finally told us."

"But she's your mother!"

"She's not my mother any longer! How could a Jew bitch be my mother?"

SARA TUVEL BERNSTEIN

The Seamstress: A Memoir of Survival

In Auschwitz the aim of the [medical] experiments was primarily to find the most expeditious way of sterilizing human beings. The results of the "research" were to be used both to advance the war against the Jews—especially the offspring of mixed marriages—and to enhance the aryan race. One of the SS physicians working on the sterilization research, Dr. Horst Schumann... conducted his experiments in the women's camp in Birkenau, sterilizing his subjects by means of X-rays.

Leni Yahil
The Holocaust: The Fate of European Jewry, 1932-1945

[THE GYNAECOLOGICAL ANATOMIST PROFESSOR DR HERMANN STIEVE (1886-1952), OF THE UNIVERSITY OF BERLIN AND THE BERLIN CHARITE HOSPITAL] IS KNOWN TO HAVE EXPLOITED WOMEN PRISONERS FOR HIS STUDIES ON THE EFFECT OF MENTAL STRESS ON THE MENSTRUAL CYCLE. THE MENTAL STRESS WAS THE WOMEN'S OWN IMPENDING EXECUTION. ON THE WOMEN'S EXECUTION STIEVE HAD THEIR PELVIC ORGANS REMOVED FOR STUDY.

WILLIAM SEIDELMAN

"Nuremberg Lamentation:
For the Forgotten Victims of Medical Science"

British Medical Journal

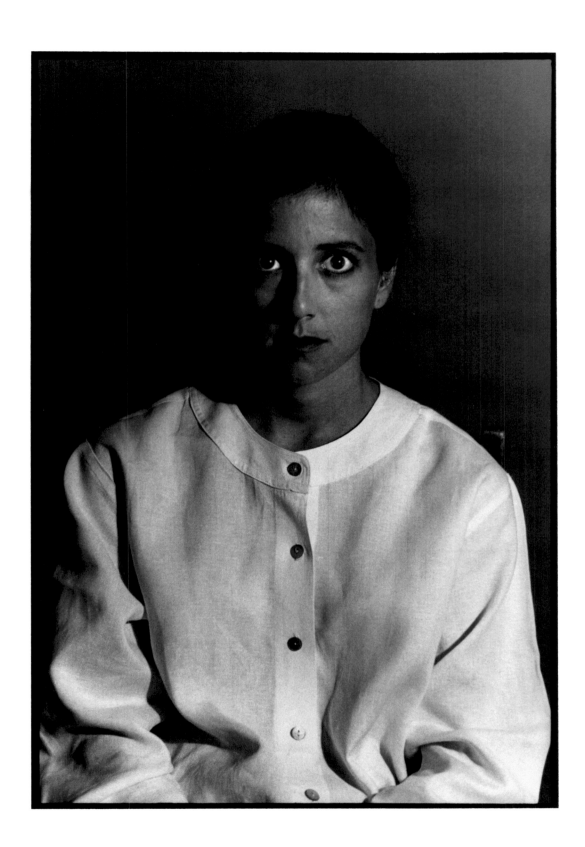

For a variety of reasons, the women's situation [at Auschwitz-Birkenau] was a good deal worse than that for the men: first, less physical endurance, coupled with work more arduous and degrading than the labors imposed on the men; the agonies of disrupted families; and above all the haunting presence of the crematoria, located right in the middle of the women's camp, inescapable, undeniable, their ungodly smoke rising from chimneys to contaminate every day and every night, every moment of respite or illusion, every dream and timorous hope.

PRIMO LEVI

Enduring Appell [roll call] was a sort of torture itself. You were strictly forbidden to move, and because the procedure lasted an eternity, it will be clear what that meant for the prisoners who, almost without exception, suffered from dysentery. In plain language, many of us just stood there with shit running down our legs, in complete agony. How easy it was to call us 'dirty smelling pigs.'

ANITA LASKER-WALLFISCH
Inherit the Truth: A Memoir of Survival and the Holocaust

"Take off your clothes!"

Her bloody hands tried to unbutton the white blouse, but didn't have the strength. Otto ripped it off with his hand. He took off his leather jacket and put it on the ground after folding it carefully. This calm, careful way of preparing for her murder upset me more than everything that followed.

Ana Novac
*The Beautiful Days of My Youth:
My Six Months in Auschwitz and Plaszow*

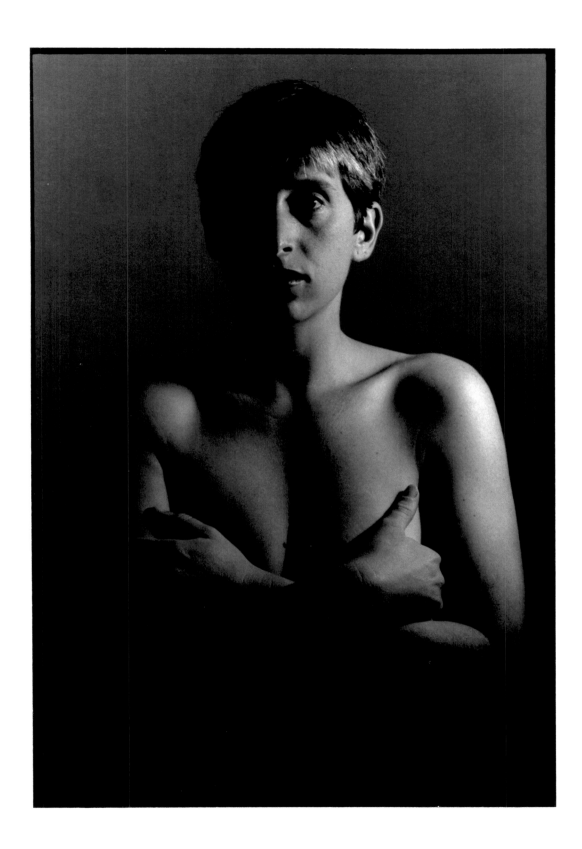

WE WERE FAIRLY NEAR THE ELECTRIFIED FENCE AND
SUDDENLY I SAW ONE WOMAN RUN UP TO IT AND GRIP
THE METAL. VIOLENTLY SHAKEN BY THE CURRENT, HER
BODY TWISTED AND SHE HUNG THERE, HER LIMBS
TWITCHING CONVULSIVELY; AGAINST THE LIGHT SHE
LOOKED LIKE A MONSTROUS SPIDER DANCING IN ITS
WEB. A FRIEND RUSHED FORWARD TO DETACH HER,
SEIZED HER, AND WAS WELDED TO HER ARMS BY THE
CURRENT, WRITHING SPASMODICALLY FROM HEAD TO
FOOT. NO ONE MOVED, THE MUSIC PLAYED ON; THE
SS LISTENED AND TALKED AMONG THEMSELVES.

FANIA FENELON
Playing for Time

NEXT TO ME, FRITZI, LOOKING UP TO WHERE THEY
WERE BURNING THE SKIES, THEN DOWN TO WHERE
THEY WERE STOKING THE FIRES AND FEEDING THE
FLAMES WITH JEWS, SAID IN A HOLLOW, FAR-AWAY
VOICE, "MY MOTHER'S IN THERE," AND AFTER THAT,
SHE NEVER SPOKE AGAIN.

SILVIA GROHS-MARTIN
Silvie

O YOU WHO KNOW

DID YOU KNOW THAT HUNGER MAKES THE EYES SPARKLE THAT THIRST DIMS

   THEM

O YOU WHO KNOW

DID YOU KNOW THAT YOU CAN SEE YOUR MOTHER DEAD

AND NOT SHED A TEAR

CHARLOTTE DELBO
Auschwitz and After

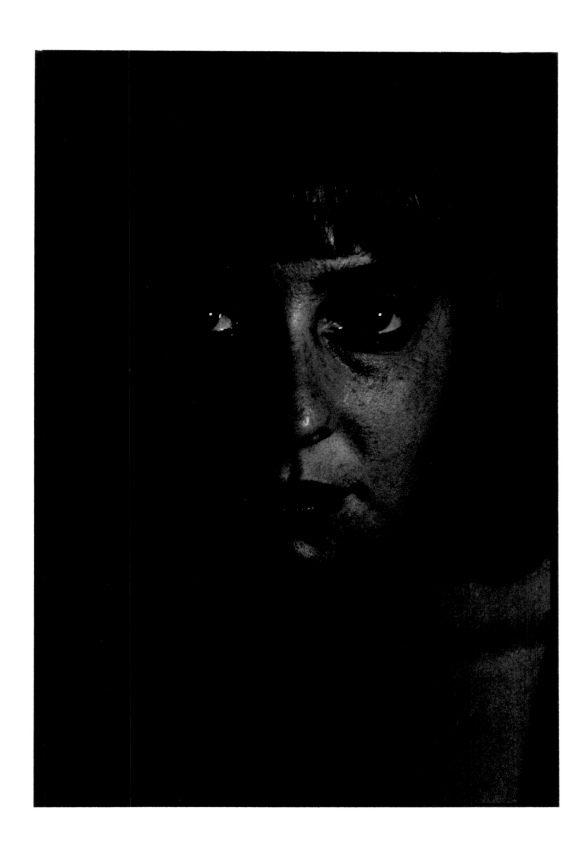

AMONG THE MANY VICTIMS OF THE HOLOCAUST WAS
THE CLASSICAL IDEA OF THE BEAUTY OF THE HUMAN
FORM. HUMILIATED MEMORY TESTIFIES TO THE EROSION
OF THAT IDEAL....

LAWRENCE L. LANGER
Holocaust Testimonies: The Ruins of Memory

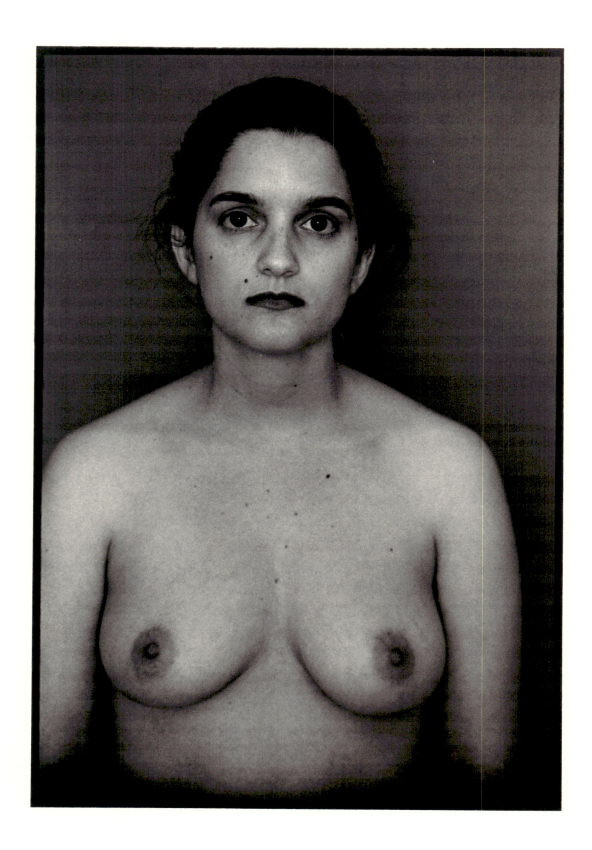

THEY WERE WAITING FOR US AND THEY SHAVED US OF OUR PUBIC HAIR, THE HAIR ON OUR HEADS, AND THE HAIR UNDER OUR ARM PITS.... BEFORE LONG WE LOOKED FOR ONE ANOTHER, BUT WE HAD DIFFICULTY RECOGNIZING OUR FRIENDS AND LOVED ONES. WHEN WE FINALLY DID, WE CRIED OUT: *GUTKA? ZOSIA? ESTA? HALUNIA? LONYA? IS THAT YOU?* WE LAUGHED HYSTERICALLY BECAUSE WE LOOKED LIKE MONKEYS.

RIVA CHIRURG
Bridge of Sorrow, Bridge of Hope

ONCE AGAIN, WE WERE SITTING ON THE BENCHES, NAKED, THE HAIR ON OUR HEADS, WHAT WAS LEFT OF IT, CUT IN LAYERS, ALL OF US HUNCHED OVER FROM THE COLD. I WAS LOOKING FOR ACQUAINTANCES AMONG THOSE TRANSFORMED FIGURES, AND TRULY, I DID NOT RECOGNIZE ANYBODY. HOW TRAGIC, AND AT THE SAME TIME, HOW COMIC, EVERYBODY LOOKED. THINK OF IT. ONCE UPON A TIME, EACH OF US WAS CAPABLE OF AWAKENING FEELINGS OF LOVE AND AFFECTION. EACH OF US ONCE HAD SOME VALUE, HER OWN WORLD OF INTIMATE DREAMS AND DESIRES.

SARA NOMBERG-PRZYTYK
Auschwitz: True Tales From a Grotesque Land

THE BREASTS BEGAN TO SAG AT FIRST AND THEN BE-
CAME VIRTUAL EMPTY SACKS.... THEN THE EMPTY
SACKS BECAME SHORTER. EVENTUALLY THE SKIN,
TOO, WAS ABSORBED AND THE BREASTS DISAPPEARED
COMPLETELY. WE WERE ALL LIKE MEN. FLAT. IN TIME
THE BONES BEGAN TO PROTRUDE AND SHRUNKEN
SKIN LAY TAUT ON EVERY POINTED BULGE.

LIVIA E. BITTON JACKSON
Elli: Coming of Age in the Holocaust

IS A LICE-FILLED BAG OF BONES A WOMAN, AN OBJECT OF DESIRE? WITH THE EXCEPTION OF A FEW—PEOPLE WORKING IN THE KITCHENS, *KAPOS*, THE HANDFUL OF WOMEN SINGLED OUT FOR GERMAN LUST—WE ALL WERE JUST SUCH BAGS OF BONES. CAN ANYONE IMAGINE A LICE-FILLED WALKING SKELETON AS A GODDESS OF LOVE?

ISABELLA LEITNER
Isabella: From Auschwitz to Freedom

IN BERGEN-BELSEN WE BEGAN TO DIE. IT WAS A SLOW PROCESS. ONE BECAME THINNER AND THINNER UNTIL ONE BECAME A SKELETON....

FELICIA WEINGARTEN

WHOEVER HAS KNOWN TRUE STARVATION KNOWS THAT HUNGER IS NOT MERELY AN AUTONOMIC ANIMALISTIC SENSATION IN THE STOMACH, BUT A NERVE-SHATTERING PAIN, AN ATTACK ON THE WHOLE PERSONALITY. HUNGER MAKES A PERSON VICIOUS AND UNDERMINES HER CHARACTER. MANY OF THE THINGS THE PRISONERS DID, THINGS THAT RIGHTLY SEEM OUTRAGEOUS AND MONSTROUS TO THE OUTSIDER, BECOME UNDERSTANDABLE AND TO A CERTAIN EXTENT EXCUSABLE WHEN SEEN FROM THE PERSPECTIVE OF STARVATION.

LUCIE ADELSBERGER
Auschwitz: A Doctor's Story

Food was the coin that paid for sexual privileges.

It would be heartless to condemn women who had to sink so low for a half crust of bread. The responsibility for the degradation of the internees rested with the camp administration.

Be that as it may, prostitution with all it lamentable consequences: venereal diseases, pimps, etc., was an ordinary phenomenon at Birkenau.

OLGA LENGYEL
Five Chimneys

BY THE HUNDREDS THEY WERE TAKEN AWAY TO UN-KNOWN DESTINATIONS. NO REPORTS WERE RECEIVED FROM THEM. A SOLDIER, DECENT BY COMPARISON, LET IT BE KNOWN THAT THE MAJORITY OF THE YOUNG GIRLS WERE SENT TO THE FRONT, AS PROSTITUTES. THE GIRLS SOON CONTRACTED VENEREAL DISEASES, AND WERE THEN BURNED ALIVE OR SHOT.

RENYA KULKIELKO
Escape from the Pit

THEN THE ORCHESTRA WAS ORDERED TO PLAY, AND THE SS MEN WOULD SING ALONG WHILE THEY CONTINUED TO DRINK, THEIR MOOD GETTING EVEN MORE BOISTEROUS. YOUNG JEWISH WOMEN WOULD BE PULLED FROM THEIR BUNKS, TAKEN AWAY SOMEWHERE, AND RAPED. RAPING JEWISH WOMEN WASN'T CONSIDERED *RASSENSCHANDE* (RACE DEFILEMENT), THEREFORE IT WAS ALLOWED.... ANY WOMAN WHO REFUSED TO GO WITH THE SS MEN WAS SAVAGELY BEATEN....

RUTH ELIAS

Triumph of Hope:
From Theresienstadt and Auschwitz to Israel

ALTHOUGH THERE ARE MANY STORIES ABOUT SEXUAL ABUSE, THEY ARE NOT EASY TO COME BY. SOME THINK IT INAPPROPRIATE TO TALK ABOUT THESE MATTERS; DISCUSSIONS ABOUT SEXUALITY DESECRATE THE MEMORIES OF THE DEAD, OR THE LIVING, OR THE HOLOCAUST ITSELF. FOR OTHERS IT IS JUST TOO DIFFICULT AND PAINFUL. STILL OTHERS THINK IT MAY BE A TRIVIAL ISSUE. ONE SURVIVOR TOLD ME THAT SHE WAS SEXUALLY ABUSED BY A NUMBER OF GENTILE MEN WHILE SHE WAS IN HIDING.... HER COMMENT ABOUT THIS WAS THAT IT "WAS NOT IMPORTANT...EXCEPT TO ME."

JOAN RINGELHEIM
"Women and the Holocaust: A Reconsideration of Research"

WHATEVER WILL BECOME OF ME? AND OF LILLI, AND ALL THE REST? IT WASN'T SO MUCH THE FEAR OF DEATH THAT PAINED ME, BUT RATHER THE GALLING FUTILITY OF THIS EXISTENCE SUSPENDED BETWEEN TWO VOIDS. HERE TODAY, GONE TOMORROW. WHAT COULD BE THE POINT OF ALL THIS SUFFERING...IN THE MIDST OF NOTHING? WAS IT POSSIBLE SOME GOD WAS LOOKING DOWN ON ME FROM ABOVE? WHY DID HE PUT ME HERE IN THE FIRST PLACE IF I WAS SIMPLY TO SUFFER AND VANISH WITHOUT A TRACE? HAD HE NO MERCY, THIS GOD?

LIANA MILLU
Smoke Over Birkenau

APATHY MIXED WITH FEAR OF THE NEXT DAY, OR
MAYBE THE NEXT WEEK, WAS WITH US CONSTANTLY.
LYING AWAKE I COULD HEAR MOANING. ONCE IN
A WHILE SOMEONE SOBBED. WHERE COULD THEY
STILL FIND TEARS?

HANNA KOHNER
Hanna and Walter: A Love Story

We needed lots of spiritual strength to keep a shred of human dignity in our dense world of humiliation and sorrow. We had many thousands of hours to contemplate our fate, our suffering, the hidden rationale behind G-d's plans, and when it all might come to an end. We wondered about the human capacity for hatred that drove the Germans and others to such depravity.

MIRIAM KUPERHAND
Shadows of Treblinka

Somehow we figure out how many Sundays we have been in camp. This tells us it is Yom Kippur, and we fast from sundown to sundown. In my heart I pray: Oh, Lord, my Lord, please help my parents and protect them until we can return home. Tell them we are alive and that we love them. Tell Mama that I know she is watching over us through your eyes. Strengthen our faith and our bodies. Let us not falter from hunger. In your name, Lord, who is my Lord.

RENA KORNREICH GELISSEN
Rena's Promise: A Story of Sisters in Auschwitz

"PEOPLE DID CARE FOR EACH OTHER. PEOPLE DID GIVE EACH OTHER MORAL SUPPORT. PEOPLE DID COMMISERATE WITH EACH OTHER AND TRIED TO HELP. THERE WAS VERY LITTLE BECAUSE PEOPLE WERE DYING AND THE SUFFERING WAS SO INTENSE THAT IT WAS VERY DIFFICULT TO GIVE STRENGTH TO SOMEONE ELSE...."

NINA K.

IT WAS AN UNWRITTEN LAW THAT SISTERS AND FRIENDS KEPT TOGETHER, SAT NEXT TO EACH OTHER, SCARCELY DARED TO LET GO OF EACH OTHER'S HANDS. ANYTHING MIGHT HAPPEN. WE DARED NOT CHALLENGE FATE BY LETTING EACH OTHER OUT OF SIGHT.

HEDI FRIED
The Road to Auschwitz: Fragments of a Life

MOST PEOPLE BEHAVED POORLY IN THE CAMPS. THEY STOLE BREAD FROM THEIR FELLOW INMATES AND RE-PORTED OTHERS TO THE KAPO WHEN IT WAS TO THEIR ADVANTAGE. LIFE WAS SO GRIM, THERE WAS SIMPLY NO ROOM FOR HEROICS.

HELEN H. WATERFORD
Commitment to the Dead

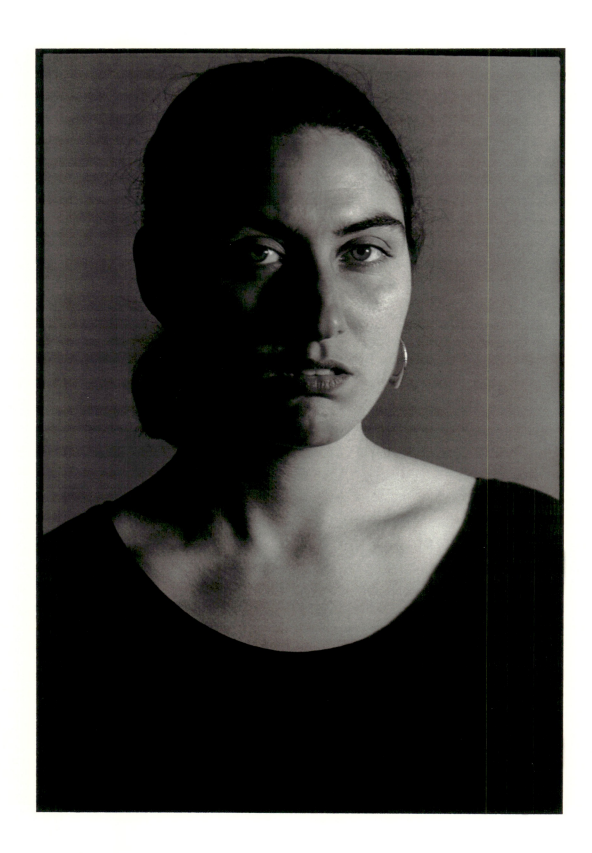

A GUN WAS IN MY HAND NOW.... NOW, IF THE ENEMY
POINTED HIS GUN ON ME, I COULD SHOOT BACK. I
HAD THE OPPORTUNITY TO AVENGE THE BLOOD OF
MY MOTHER, MY FATHER, MY SISTERS, MY BROTHER
AND MY SISTER'S TWO CHILDREN. I WAS NOT AFRAID
OF BEING KILLED. RESPONSIBLE ONLY FOR MYSELF, I
NO LONGER HAD MUCH TO LOSE EXCEPT MY LIFE.

FAYE SCHULMAN
A Partisan's Memoir: Woman of the Holocaust

"Little Wanda with the Braids," Niuta Teitelboim, was a self-appointed executioner. She walked into the Gestapo office, shot an officer and walked out with a smile. She repeated it in another Gestapo officers house, shooting him in bed. In the Ghetto she organized the women, teaching them how to use weapons.

Vera Laska
*Women in the Resistance and in the Holocaust:
The Voices of Eyewitnesses*

She left and reentered the ghetto several times knowing each time she went in that she might never get out. She became the movement's most important liaison. She was able to make her way through her neverending chain of assignments by using her articulateness and voluptuous beauty with the confidence of a woman supremely aware of her charms. None of the casual acquaintances she met in her travels suspected that Hela was smuggling weapons—that she had two Brownings hanging under her loose sports coat and three hand weapons and a few clips of cartridges in her new bag.

GUSTA DAVIDSON DRAENGER
Justyna's Narrative

[MALA ZIMETBAUM] STOLE AN SS UNIFORM AND GER-
MAN DOCUMENTS TELLING OF THE SLAUGHTER AT THE
DEATH CAMP. SHE ESCAPED, ONLY TO BE RECAPTURED
AND SENT BACK TO AUSCHWITZ. THE NAZIS PARADED
HER IN FRONT OF THE WHOLE CAMP. SUDDENLY, SHE
BEGAN TO SLASH HER OWN WRIST WITH A RAZOR....
"DON'T BE AFRAID, GIRLS," SHE YELLED, "THEIR END IS
NEAR. I AM CERTAIN OF THIS. I KNOW. I WAS FREE."

SEYMOUR ROSSEL
The Holocaust: The World and the Jews, 1933-1945

October 23 [1943]. Some 1,800 Polish Jews arrive in Auschwitz from Bergen-Belsen. The women are taken to Crematorium II, where they are ordered to undress. One woman, a beautiful young dancer named Franceska Mann, flings part of her clothing at the head of SS Staff Sergeant Schillinger, grabs his revolver, and shoots him twice. She also shoots SS Sergeant Emmerich. Other women attack the SS men with their bare hands.

Carol Rittner and John K. Roth
Different Voices: Women and the Holocaust

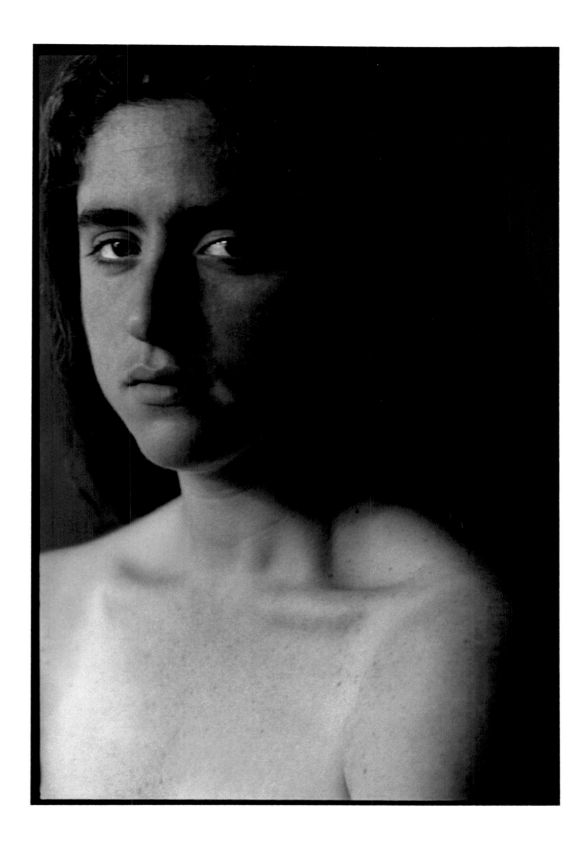

[THE GESTAPO AND S.S.] KNEW SHE WAS JEWISH, BUT THEY KNEW ALSO THAT SHE WAS A BRITISH PARATROOPER WHO HAD COME TO FIGHT THEM. HAVING BEEN TAUGHT FOR YEARS THAT JEWS NEVER FIGHT BACK, THAT THEY WILL ACCEPT THE VILEST TREATMENT, THEY WERE TAKEN ABACK BY HER COURAGE.

YOEL PALGI
"How She Fell"
Hannah Senesh: Her Life and Diary

THE JEWS [OF THE GHETTO] DEFENDED THEMSELVES VALIANTLY. ON THE ROOFS OF HOUSES NOT AS YET ENVELOPED BY FLAMES, BOYS MANNING MACHINE GUNS COULD BE SEEN THROUGH THE SMOKE, AS THROUGH A HEAVY FOG. GIRLS FOUGHT HEROICALLY, ARMED WITH PISTOLS AND BOTTLES OF EXPLOSIVES.

RENYA KULKIELKO
Escape from the Pit

By honoring the heroes, don't scholars end up dishonoring the ones who were not heroic, and sometimes ignoring the regime that engineered a system deliberately designed to make heroism virtually impossible? To expect heroism from victims or to romantically attribute it to them is to treat the Holocaust as if it were a character test, rather than a program of systematic dehumanization.

Naomi Seidman
"Toward a Feminist Holocaust Studies"

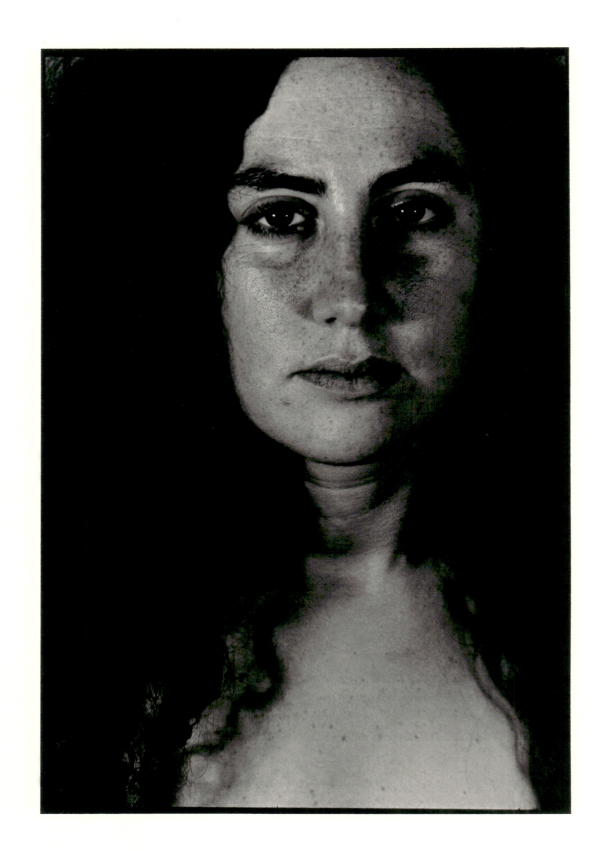

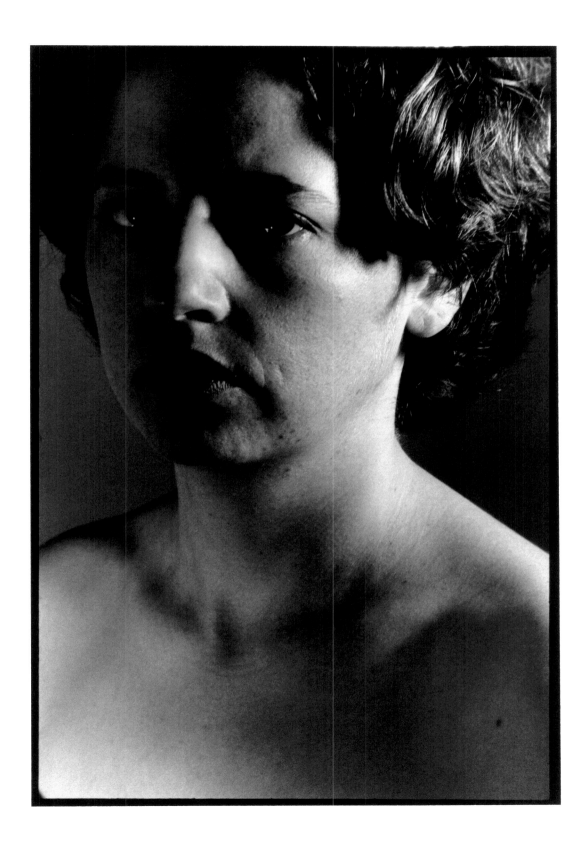

To a mouth

for which it was a thousandword,

lost—

I lost a word

that was left to me:

Sister.

PAUL CELAN
The Sluice

ACKNOWLEDGMENTS

My heartfelt appreciation to the following women whose
participation made this project possible:

Leila Alpers

Rachel Arthur

Leslie Bauer

Susan Bessler

Amy Blechman

Jill Blumberg

Tamar Cohen

Anna Davidson

Tamara Doering

Laura Doldner

Lisa Egert

Kaila Flexer

Lily Robert Foley

Michal Friedlander

Lauren Goldberg

Leslie Goldberg

Lara Goldstone

Amanda Nowinski Gould

Molly Gould

Shelly Grossman

Judith Hahn

April Hunter

Cecily Hunter

Deborah Jaffe

Andrea Liss

Lisa Loeb

Andrea Michaels

Ayala Mirandé

Elisabeth Oppenheimer

Andrea Raider

Susan Reider

Elaine Reiter

Evelyn Robert

Yael Robson

Catherine Ross

Lauren Ross

Naomi Schegloff

Sharone Sheffer

Grace Shohet

Michelle Sicula

Amie Siegel

Jessica Silberstein

Rachel Silberstein

Beth Silverstein

Jocelyn Sperling

Iryce Starr

Rachel Steinhart

Eve Weiss

Pamela Wool

Sara Yanowitz

My gratitude to the following for their support and encouragement:

Gay Block, Jean Caslin, Bill Cirocco, Michael Dawson, James Delano, Natasha Egan, John Felstiner, Mary Lowenthal Felstiner, Tom Ferentz, Nancy Fewkes, Marnie Gillette, Michael Goldberg, Ted Hartwell, Bettina Leong, Barbara Levine, Maria Louise Oberem, Alison O'Brien, Rabbi Stephen Pearce, Jack Ross, Barbara Ross, Susan Schwartzenberg, Bill Shays, Karen and Arnold Stillman, Richard Superfine, Bill Surkis, Pat Thompson, Trent Thornley, Ellen Ullman, Mrs. Jack M. Ullman, Louise Victor, Jan Watten, Sharon Wickham, and Connie Wolf.

REFERENCES

The authors or publishers of the texts quoted herein retain exclusive ownership in the copyright of those texts. Those wishing to use them in any other context should contact the publishers of the original materials directly.

Adelsberger, Lucie. *Auschwitz: A Doctor's Story*, trans. Susan Ray. Boston: Northeastern University Press, 1995. Page 45.

Adler, David A. *We Remember the Holocaust*. New York: Henry Holt and Company, Inc., 1995. Page 74.

Bernstein, Sara Tuvel. *The Seamstress: A Memoir of Survival*. New York: G. P. Putnam's Sons, 1997. Page 152.

Borowski, Tadeusz. "Farewell To Maria," trans. Tadeusz Pióro. In *Holocaust Poetry*, compiled and introduced by Hilda Schiff. New York: St. Martin's Griffin, 1996. Page 120.

Celan, Paul "The Sluice," trans. John Felstiner. In *Paul Celan: Poet, Survivor, Jew*, John Felstiner. New Haven: Yale University Press, 1995. Page 162.

Chirurg, Riva. *Bridge of Sorrow, Bridge of Hope*, ed. Rebecca Camhi Fromer. Berkeley: Judah L. Magnes Museum, 1994. Page 126.

Delbo, Charlotte. *Auschwitz and After*, trans. Rosette C. Lamont. New Haven: Yale University Press, 1995. Page 11.

Draenger, Gusta Davidson. *Justyna's Narrative*, trans. Roslyn Hirsch and David H. Hirsch. Amherst: University of Massachussetts Press, 1996. Page 70.

Edvardson, Cordelia. *Burned Child Seeks Fire*, trans. Joel Agee. Boston: Beacon Press, 1997. Page 68.

Elias, Ruth. *Triumph of Hope: From Theresienstadt and Auschwitz to Israel*, trans. Margot Bettauer Dembo. New York: John Wiley and Sons, Inc., 1998. Page 120.

Felstiner, Mary Lowenthal. *To Paint Her Life: Charlotte Salomon in the Nazi Era*. New York: HarperPerennial, 1995. Page 207.

Fenelon, Fania. *Playing for Time*, trans. Judith Landry. Syracuse: Syracuse University Press, 1997. Pages 192–193.

Fried, Hedi. *The Road to Auschwitz: Fragments of a Life*, trans. Michael Meyer. Lincoln, Neb.: University of Nebraska Press, 1996. Page 138.

Gelissen, Rena Kornreich. *Rena's Promise: A Story of Sisters in Auschwitz*. With Heather Dune Macadam. Boston: Beacon Press, 1995. Pages 108–109.

Goldenberg, Myrna. "Different Horrors, Same Hell: Women Remembering the Holocaust." In *Thinking the Unthinkable,* ed. Roger S. Gottlieb. Mahwah, N. J.: Paulist Press, 1990. Page 155.

Grohs-Martin, Silvia. *Sylvie.* New York: Welcome Rain Publishers, 2000. Page 238.

Hitler, Adolf. *Mein Kampf,* trans. Ralph Manheim. Boston: Houghton Mifflin Company, 1996. Page 52.

Jackson, Livia E. Bitton. *Elli: Coming Of Age in the Holocaust.* New York: New York Times Books, 1980. Page 81.

K., Nina. Quoted in *Love Carried Me Home: Women Surviving Auschwitz,* Joy Erlichman Miller. Deerfield Beach, Fla.: Simcha Press, 2000. Page 35.

Kohner, Hanna and Walter. *Hanna and Walter: A Love Story.* New York: Berkeley Books, 1997. Page 139.

Kulkielko, Renya. *Escape From the Pit.* New York: Sharon Books, 1947. Pages 22 and 93-94.

Kuperhand, Miriam and Saul. *Shadows of Treblinka.* Urbana, Ill: University of Illinois Press, 1998. Page 61.

Langer, Lawrence L. *Holocaust Testimonies: The Ruins of Memory.* New Haven: Yale University Press, 1991. Pages xv and 101.

Laska, Vera, ed. *Women In the Resistance and In the Holocaust: The Voices of Eyewitnesses.* Westport, Conn: Greenwood Press, 1983. Page 10.

Lasker-Wallfisch, Anita. *Inherit the Truth: A Memoir of Survival and the Holocaust.* New York: St. Martin's Press, 2000. Page 73.

Leitner, Isabella and Irving A. *Isabella: From Auschwitz to Freedom.* New York: Anchor Books, 1994. Page 127.

Lengyel, Olga. *Five Chimneys.* Chicago: Academy Chicago Publishers, 1995. Page 196.

Levi, Primo, "Introduction." In *Smoke Over Birkenau,* by Liana Millu, trans. Lynne Sharon Schwartz. Evanston, Ill: Northwestern University Press, 1997. Page 7.

Millu, Liana. *Smoke Over Birkenau,* trans. Lynne Sharon Schwartz. Evanston, Ill: Northwestern University Press, 1997. Page 44.

Nomberg-Przytyk, Sara. *Auschwitz: True Tales From a Grotesque Land,* trans. Roslyn Hirsch, eds. Eli Pfefferkorn and David H. Hirsch. Chapel Hill: The University of North Carolina Press, 1985. Page 14.

Novac, Ana. *The Beautiful Days of My Youth: My Six Months in Auschwitz and Plaszow,* trans. George L. Newman. New York: Henry Holt and Company, 1997. Page 150.

Palgi, Yoel. "How She Fell," In *Hannah Senesh: Her Life and Diary,* trans. Marta Cohn. London: Sphere Books Limited, 1973. Page 185.

Perl, Gisella. *I Was A Doctor In Auschwitz.* New York: Arno Press, 1979. Page 80.

Ringelheim, Joan. "Women and the Holocaust: A Reconsideration of Research." *Signs: Journal of Women in Culture and Society 10* (1985). Chicago: University of Chicago Press. Page 745.

Ringelheim, Joan. "Thoughts About Women and the Holocaust." In *Thinking the Unthinkable,* ed. Roger S. Gottlieb. Mahwah, N. J.: Paulist Press, 1990. Page 146.

Rittner, Carol and John K. Roth. "Chronology." In *Different Voices: Women and the Holocaust,* ed. and with an introduction by Carol Rittner and John K. Roth. New York: Paragon House, 1993. Page 31.

Rossel, Seymour. *The Holocaust: The World and The Jews, 1933-1945.* West Orange, N.J.: Behrman House, Inc., 1992. Page 127.

Schulman, Faye. *A Partisan's Memoir: Woman of the Holocaust.* With Sarah Silberstein Swartz. Toronto: Second Story Press, 1995. Page 99.

Seidelman, William. "Nuremberg Lamentation: For the Forgotten Victims of Medical Science." *British Medical Journal*, Vol. 313, No 7070, 7 December 1996: Page 1465.

Seidman, Naomi. "Toward A Feminist Holocaust Studies." Unpublished Paper. By permission of the author.

Waterford, Helen H. *Commitment to the Dead.* Frederick, Col.: Renaissance House Publishers, 1987. Page 82.

Weingarten, Felicia. "Felicia Weingarten, Lodz, Poland." In *Witnesses to the Holocaust: An Oral History,* ed. Rhoda G. Lewin. Boston: Twayne Publishers, 1990. Page 79.

Yahil, Leni. *The Holocaust: the Fate of European Jewry, 1932–1945*, trans. Ina Friedman and Haya Galai. New York: Oxford University Press, 1991. Page 369.

Edited and designed by Elliot Ross

Prepress and print management by JB Imaging, 833 Market Street, Suite 488
San Francisco, California 94103, (415) 896-1886

Typesetting by Richard Zybert Graphics, San Francisco, California

This book is limited to numbered copies 1–500.
Each book is signed and numbered by Elliot Ross.

This is number *424*

Elliot Ross was born in Chicago. He received a Master of Fine Arts degree from the San Francisco Art Intitute in 1971. His work has been exhibited widely and is in collections in the United States and abroad, including those of the Bibliothéque Nationale, Paris; the San Francisco Museum of Modern Art; and the Art Museum of the University of New Mexico in Albuquerque. He lives in San Francisco.

Ellen Ullman is the author of *The Bug: A Novel* (Nan A. Talese/Doubleday, 2003) and the memoir *Close to the Machine: Technophilia and Its Discontents* (City Lights, 1997). Her essays and opinion pieces about the social effects of technology have appeared in *Harper's, Salon, Wired, The New York Times,* and *The Washington Post.* She is currently a contributing editor at The American Scholar.